I0112062

This Book
Belongs To

AWAKE ALL NIGHT!

By Cameron Pendergraft

Illustrated by Jennifer Tipton Cappoen

Text copyright 2022 by Cameron Pendergraft. Illustrations copyright 2022 by Jennifer Tipton Cappoen. All rights reserved. No part of this book may be reproduced or transmitted in any form or by any means, electronic or mechanical, including photography, recording, or any information storage and retrieval system, without permission in writing from the publisher. The only exceptions are brief excerpts and reviews.

Author: Cameron Pendergraft
Cover Designer and Illustrator: Jennifer Tipton Cappoen
Editor: Lynn Bemer Coble

PCKids is an imprint of **Paws and Claws Publishing, LLC.**
1589 Skeet Club Road, Suite 102 #175
High Point, NC 27265
www.PawsandClawsPublishing.com
info@pawsandclawspublishing.com

ISBN # 978-1-946198-30-3
Printed in the United States

Dedication

"For my grandchildren,
Molly, Lelia, Macey, Rebie, and Louis.
You inspire these stories."

My mom told me that when I turned nine years old,
she would let me have a friend over to spend the night.
A *sleepover!*

She added that my guest and I would be allowed to
"camp out" in my playroom. I liked that idea.

I was thrilled!

Last year I was eight.

I could only count three times in my entire life when I had slept anywhere other than somewhere we had gone on vacation or were at home.

Once, Susan invited me to stay over. I was seven.
Her mother *made* us eat *green beans. Gross!*
I'm pretty sure that was what caused me to wet her bed.
I cried a lot until my dad came to get me.

My second sleepover was at Stacy's house.
But her little brother threw up as soon as I got there.
I had to leave before we even had a chance to put on our pajamas!

My third sleepover was at our next-door neighbors' house. My brother had to come too. My dad was having his appendix out, and my mom was going to be at the hospital with him super late.

I don't really like to count that time. Plus our neighbors are just weird.

I was three-and-a-half when my little brother was born.
While Dad was at the hospital with my mom, my grandparents
came to stay at our house.

Not long after that, my grandparents told my mom that they thought I'd enjoy some special time alone with them. I started going by myself to spend the night at their house. That was the best because I got to eat all the ice cream I wanted, stay up late, and fall asleep on their couch!

Exactly one day after my ninth birthday,
I reminded my mom about her promise.

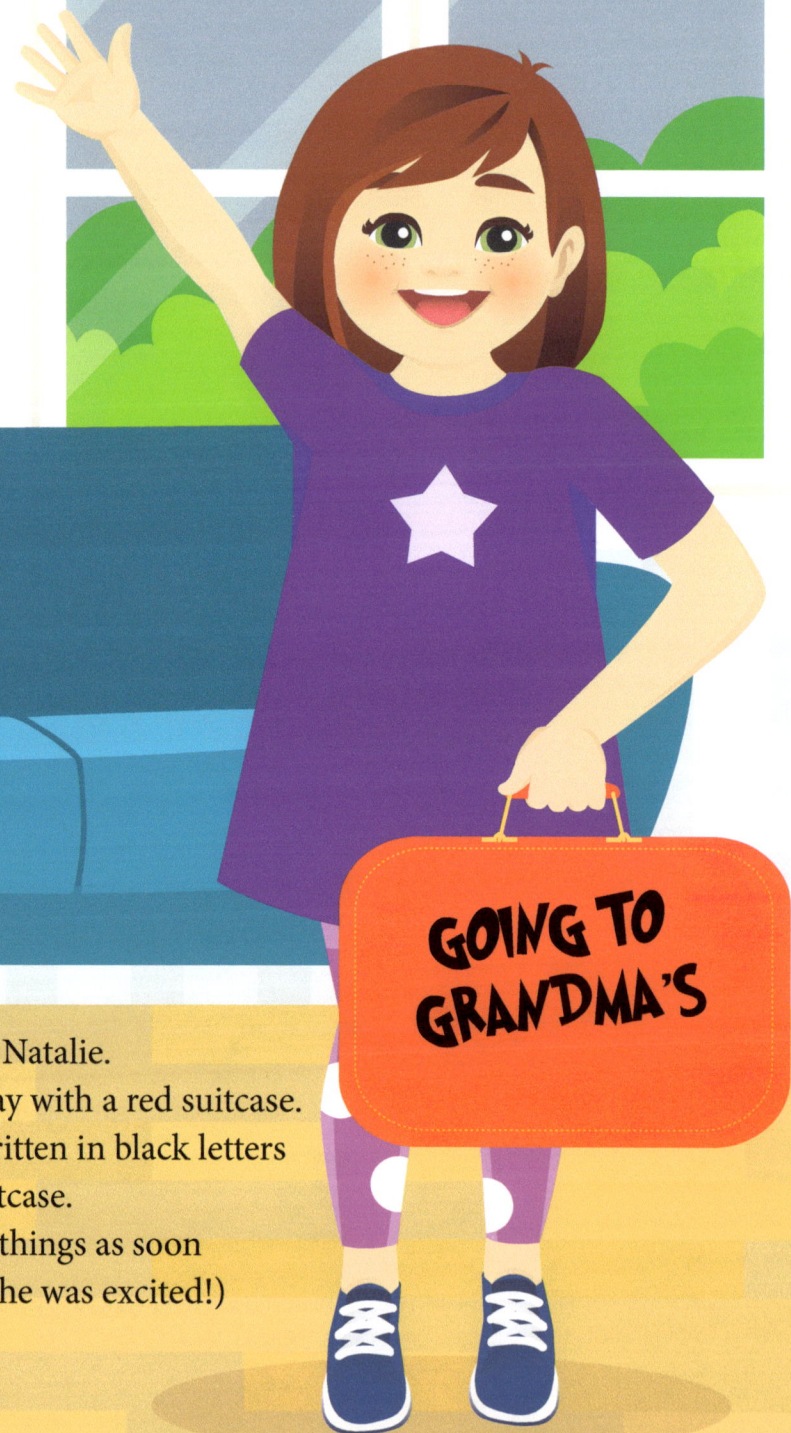

I invited my best friend Natalie.
She arrived at my house on the big day with a red suitcase.
"GOING TO GRANDMA'S" was written in black letters
on the side of her suitcase.
Natalie wanted to unpack her things as soon
as she came inside my house. (She was excited!)

GOING TO GRANDMA'S

In her suitcase were two books (one with chapters),
her toothbrush and toothpaste, clean undies, her
nightgown, and an orange washcloth.
(I guess I forgot to mention to Natalie that
we had plenty of washcloths.)

My dad called in a cheese pizza while Natalie and I took a bubble bath.
We dunked our heads in the water to see who could stay under the longest.
We may have sloshed a bit on the bathroom floor.
Luckily Mom didn't notice when she brought us our towels.
Natalie did use her orange washcloth.

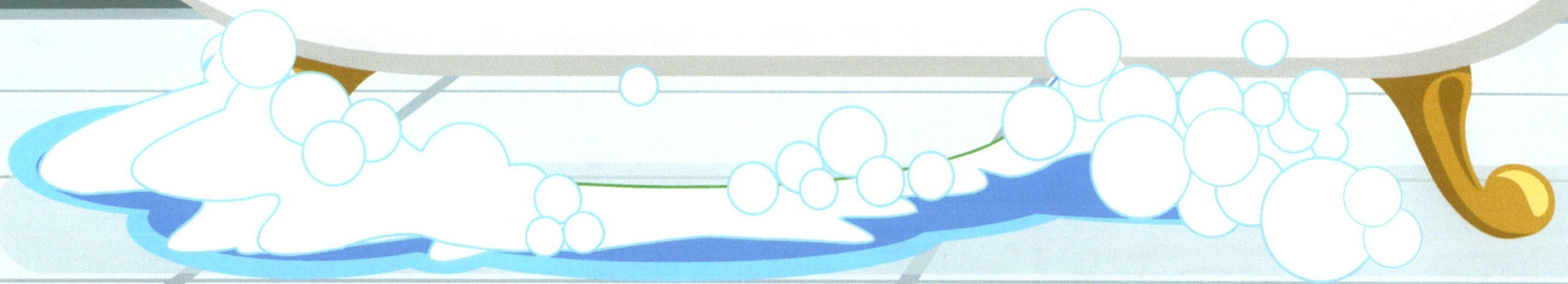

My dad let us sit on the floor in the family room
while we ate our pizza.
We watched our favorite television program.

Natalie spilled pizza sauce on the carpet.
I slid the pizza box over the stain
so no one could see it.

At around 8 o'clock, Mom gathered lots of books,
paper, crayons, scissors, and tape.
She led us to the playroom.

She also laid out two sheets,
two pillows, and a quilt on the floor.
She brought us a plate of oatmeal
cookies and two cups of milk.

meow

Natalie and I made a long collage
of pictures. We taped them
across the playroom wall.
Natalie drew the best flowers.
I drew lots of cats and houses.

After a little while, Mom came back and suggested that we lie down and look at books. She took away the paper, crayons, scissors, tape, and food.

Then she said, "I'll check on you girls in a few."

Mom looked a little tired.

Natalie said that when my mom came back, we should pretend to be asleep. I had the feeling that if I closed my eyes for one minute, I *would* be asleep.

We talked and tried to see whose arm was the longest. I told Natalie I didn't like to wear rings, and she told me she loved to wear rings.

We tried to think of the names of everyone we knew and their addresses. We made lists in our heads of our favorite books and songs.

After we did that, I asked Natalie if she wanted to go to sleep.

"*No!*" she exclaimed. "Let's see if we can *stay awake all night!*"

A long time passed. We had rearranged our sheets for the third time when we heard my mom's footsteps coming strong.

She didn't look very happy when she got to the open playroom door.

She knelt down beside us and suggested a bedtime story.
(There was no way we could have been prepared for the
horrible story she began to tell.)
The story went like this. When she was nine years old,
she went to a sleepover at a friend's house.
Her friend's name was Dana. Dana decided that it would be
fun if the two of them tried to stay awake all night.
(This sounded familiar.)

"There are three things a little girl must have in order to grow up to be healthy and strong. Those three things are love, food, and sleep." Mom was getting a little bit off track as she told her story.

But I understood her point, because she was looking directly at me when she said that. Then she went on. She explained that Dana did stay awake all that night. My mom couldn't stay awake and fell asleep.

The next morning when she woke up, Dana wasn't in bed! Mom ran downstairs to find Dana with her parents at their kitchen table. Dana had a horrible case of *hiccups!* According to my mom, the hiccups would not stop.

Mom looked down as she spoke and added sadly, "Poor Dana. She still has the hiccups. To this very day." (I wonder about that.)

LOVE! . . . . FOOD! .

SLEEP!

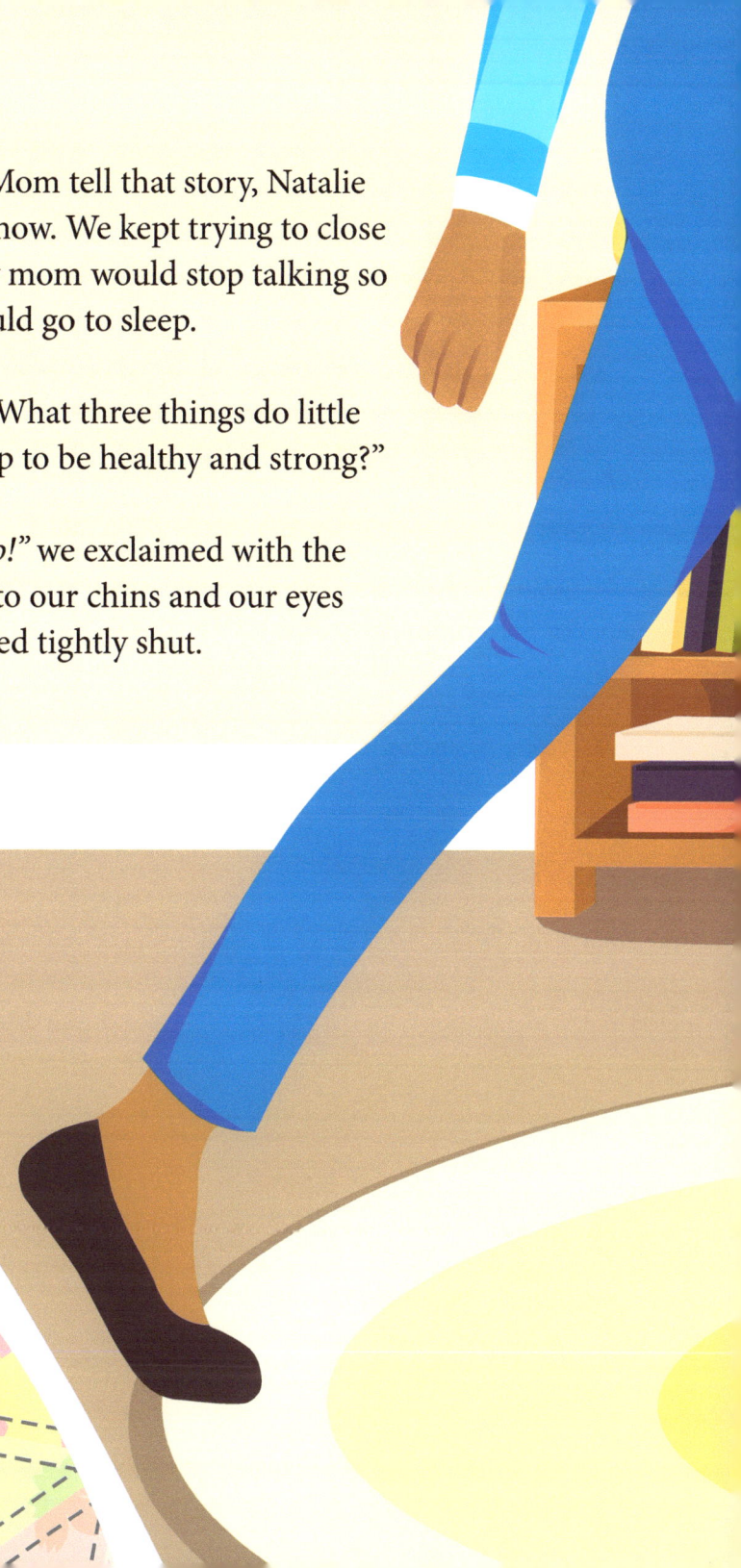

After listening to Mom tell that story, Natalie and I lay as still as snow. We kept trying to close our eyes, hoping my mom would stop talking so we could go to sleep.

But Mom asked, "What three things do little girls need to grow up to be healthy and strong?"

"Love! Food! Sleep!" we exclaimed with the sheets pulled up to our chins and our eyes squeezed tightly shut.

Mom's bedtime story worked.

The next thing I remembered was waking up with Natalie's leg on my back and the morning sun in my face.

One day in the future I may have a little girl who wants to have a friend come to our home for a sleepover. The girls may even think it would be a fun idea to *stay awake all night!*

And I'll have to be sure to tell them the old hiccup bedtime story.

I wonder if Dana
still has the
hiccups?

The

End

About the Author

Cameron, a retired preschool teacher, lives in Oxford, North Carolina, with her husband, a dog, and two cats.

Books are available at
Amazon.com and
BarnesandNoble.com

Other Books by Cameron Pendergraft

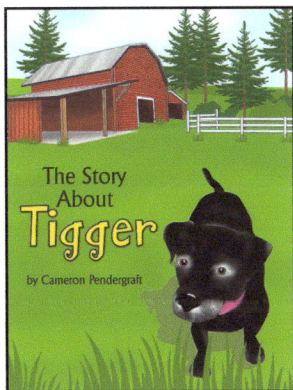

The Story About Tigger

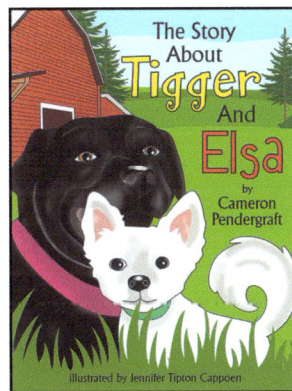

The Story About Tigger And Elsa

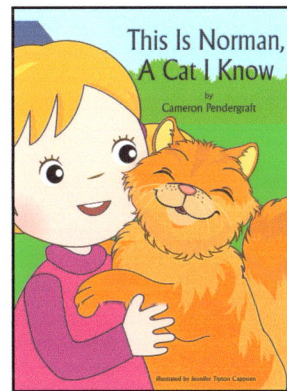

This Is Norman, A Cat I Know

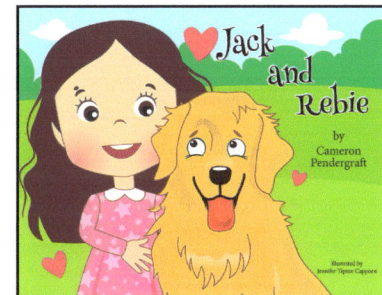

Jack and Rebie

www.ingramcontent.com/pod-product-compliance
Lightning Source LLC
LaVergne TN
LVHW070909080426

835513LV00004B/117

9 781946 198303